FLASH FORWARD MATH

Written by **Kathryn O'Dell**

Illustrations by **John Haslam**

Flash Kids
A Division of Barnes & Noble
122 Fifth Ave
New York, NY 10011

ISBN: 978-1-4114-0641-4

Please submit all inquiries to FlashKids@bn.com

Printed and bound in Canada

Lot #:
7 9 11 13 12 10 8
02/13

Dear Parent,

Math can be one of the most difficult subjects for young learners. Your child may not fully grasp concepts such as adding fractions, graphing ordered pairs, or calculating an object's area—even with a great math teacher and a thorough math textbook. Here to help at home are almost 100 pages of short drills and fun games that will reinforce all math skills taught in the fifth grade.

This colorful workbook focuses on your child's competence in multiplication, long division, rounding, percentages, graphing, fractions, and decimals. He or she will also get practice with triangle types, estimating, linear functions, volume, area, and perimeter. Additionally, activities with tables and charts keep your child engaged.

The activities are designed for your child to handle alone, but you can read along and help with any troublesome concepts. Together you can check answers at the back of the workbook, and you should always give praise and encouragement for his or her effort. In addition, try to find ways to show your child how these number skills apply to everyday situations. For example, ask him or her to multiply or divide simple household objects, such as crayons or magnets; make a table to show the family's weekly schedule; identify and count triangle types spotted during a car trip or walk around the neighborhood; or determine the correct bills and coins needed to buy an item at a store. Use your imagination!

Adding Ants

Solve the problems.

1. 500
+ 420

2. 6,000
+ 1,040

3. 555
+ 721

4. 789
+ 1,223

5. 10,452
+ 678

6. 2,344
+ 12,567

7. 7,230
+ 8,000

8. 51,000
+ 42,300

9. 33,557
+ 29,886

10. 66,700
+ 72,660

11. 86,340
+ 90,000

12. 200,000
+ 600,000

13. 345,500
+ 129,520

14. 560,346
+ 601,240

Counting Critters

Look at the chart and solve the problems.

Insect	Number of species in the world
praying mantis	2,000
dragonfly	5,000
ant	9,500
grasshopper	20,000
fly	120,000
beetle	360,000

1. How many species of ants and dragonflies are there in the world?

_____

2. How many species of grasshoppers and praying mantises are there?

_____

3. How many species of beetles and praying mantises are there?

_____

4. The Science Lab has to study all the species of flies and all the species of ants. How many species do they have to study in all?

_____

5. How many species of beetles, grasshoppers, and ants are there in all?

_____

Subtracting Stars

Solve the problems.

1. 940
  − 66

2. 459
  − 129

3. 795
  − 343

4. 1,260
  − 720

5. 2,556
  − 421

6. 3,498
  − 567

7. 6,700
  − 4,300

8. 9,342
  − 6,294

9. 7,331
  − 5,999

10. 21,908
  − 4,000

11. 32,560
  − 1,233

12. 50,629
  − 17,000

13. 68,432
  − 29,330

14. 1,000,000
  − 50,240

Solar System Subtraction

Look at the chart to find out what the scientist at Science Lab saw. Then solve the problems.

Scientist	Number of stars seen	Number of asteroids seen
Dr. Look	70,000	5,233
Dr. Pluto	62,525	6,788
Dr. Stellar	86,774	3,420

1. How many more stars than asteroids did Dr. Look see?

_____

2. How many more stars did Dr. Look see than Dr. Pluto?

_____

3. How many more stars than asteroids did Dr. Stellar see?

_____

4. How many more asteroids did Dr. Pluto see than Dr. Look?

_____

5. How many more stars did Dr. Stellar see than Dr. Look?

_____

Round off!

Round the number and choose the correct path.

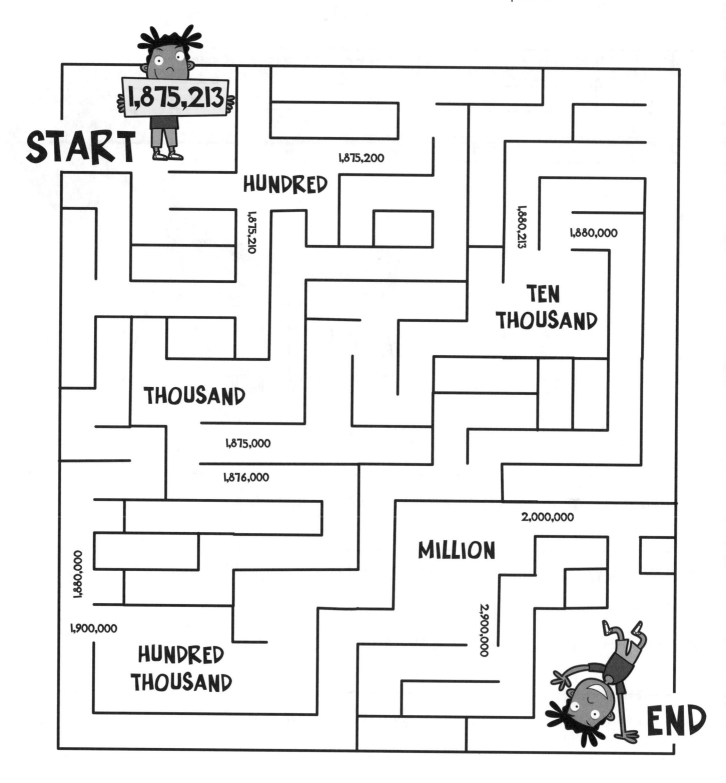

START

1,875,213

1,875,200

HUNDRED

1,875,210

1,880,213

1,880,000

TEN
THOUSAND

THOUSAND

1,875,000

1,876,000

2,000,000

MILLION

1,880,000

2,900,000

1,900,000

HUNDRED
THOUSAND

END

Decimal Round Up

Round the numbers to the nearest tenth, hundredth, and thousand. The first one is done for you.

	tenth	hundredth	thousandth
1. 10.2225	10.2	10.22	10.223
2. 9.7268			
3. 21.0561			
4. 404.8826			
5. 32.9087			
6. 212.6710			
7. 4.6792			
8. 15.0015			
9. 255.7173			
10. 99.9388			

Round Robin

Add the numbers. Then find the answers rounded to the nearest hundred, thousand, and ten thousand in the puzzle. Hint: Answers can go across or down. A number can be used in more than one answer.

1.   6,772
     + 31,456

2.   43,005
     + 14,678

3.   22,112
     + 61,346

3	5	8	0	0	0	7	2
8	9	3	8	2	0	0	0
0	8	6	3	7	3	6	9
0	4	9	5	5	6	0	8
0	1	3	0	7	9	0	3
9	7	9	0	7	4	0	0
8	0	0	0	0	8	0	0
6	5	6	4	0	0	0	0

Robin Round Two

Subtract the numbers. Then match them to the worms with the correct round numbers to the nearest hundred, thousand, and ten thousand.

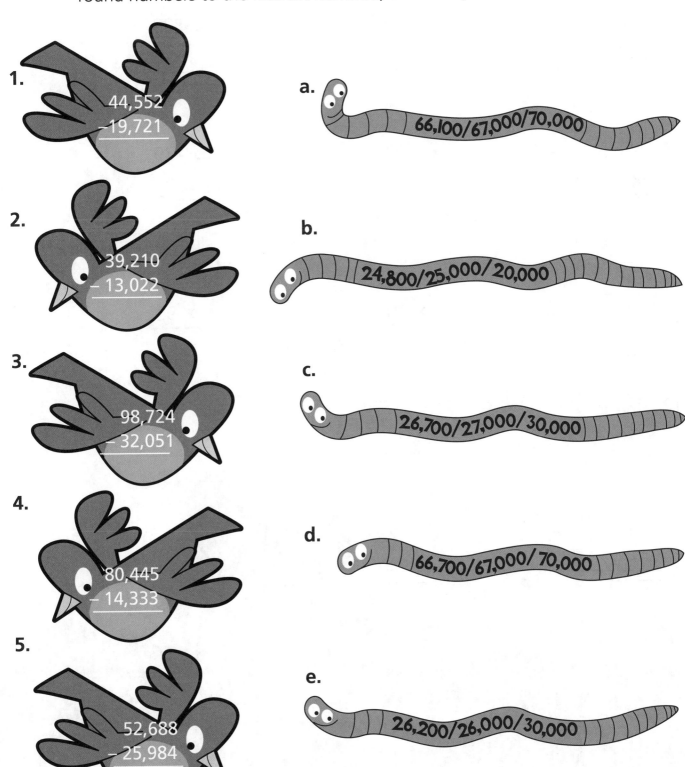

1.
44,552
− 19,721

a. 66,100/67,000/70,000

2.
39,210
− 13,022

b. 24,800/25,000/20,000

3.
98,724
− 32,051

c. 26,700/27,000/30,000

4.
80,445
− 14,333

d. 66,700/67,000/70,000

5.
52,688
− 25,984

e. 26,200/26,000/30,000

An Ocean of Numbers

Solve the problems.

1. 453
  × 5

2. 199
  × 8

3. 829
  × 6

4. 456
  × 0

5. 13
  × 12

6. 39
  × 21

7. 53
  × 42

8. 134
  × 10

9. 268
  × 93

10. 472
  × 76

11. 823
  × 48

12. 134
  × 167

13. 431
  × 205

14. 623
  × 340

Sea Life Surprises

Read and solve the problems.

1. A killer whale eats 500 pounds of food a day. How many pounds of food does it eat in a week?

_____

2. Sea turtles lay eggs in holes on the beach. They lay 70 eggs in one hole. There are 36 holes with eggs in them on the beach. How many eggs are on the beach?

_____

3. One pound of seaweed has 29 calories. How many calories do 16 pounds of seaweed have?

_____

4. A crab has ten legs. If there are 489 crabs, how many legs are there altogether?

_____

5. A small dolphin weighs 330 pounds. How much do 62 small dolphins weigh altogether?

_____

Dive Deep

Solve the problems. Then draw lines to connect the matching numbers on the page.

1.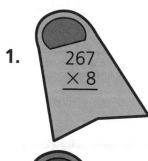
$$\begin{array}{r} 267 \\ \times\ 8 \\ \hline \end{array}$$

a.  1,134

2.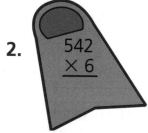
$$\begin{array}{r} 542 \\ \times\ 6 \\ \hline \end{array}$$

b. 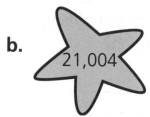 21,004

3.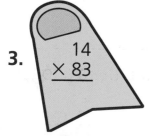
$$\begin{array}{r} 14 \\ \times\ 83 \\ \hline \end{array}$$

c.  2,136

4.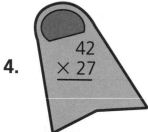
$$\begin{array}{r} 42 \\ \times\ 27 \\ \hline \end{array}$$

d.  21,049

5.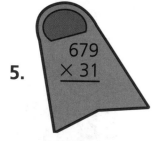
$$\begin{array}{r} 679 \\ \times\ 31 \\ \hline \end{array}$$

e. 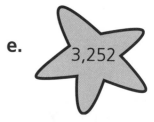 3,252

6.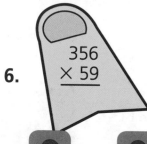
$$\begin{array}{r} 356 \\ \times\ 59 \\ \hline \end{array}$$

f.  1,162

Hit a Homerun

Solve the problems. Some of the answers have remainders.

1. $5\overline{)605}$

2. $3\overline{)156}$

3. $4\overline{)219}$

4. $6\overline{)902}$

5. $8\overline{)349}$

6. $9\overline{)648}$

7. $5\overline{)1,500}$

8. $3\overline{)3,296}$

9. $4\overline{)2,337}$

10. $8\overline{)7,800}$

11. $12\overline{)562}$

12. $29\overline{)754}$

13. $43\overline{)860}$

14. $80\overline{)562}$

Let's Go to the Ball Game!

Read and solve the problems.

1. Danny, Linda, and Raoul play baseball. Their total number of hits for the summer is 126. They each got an equal number of hits. How many hits did they each get?

_____

2. Jonathan plays basketball. He scored 336 points in seven games. He scored an equal number of points in each game. How many points did he score in each game?

_____

3. A basketball game has four quarters. Each quarter lasts an equal amount of time. A game lasts for 40 minutes. How long is each quarter?

_____

4. Lindsey has three friends. They went to an equal number of soccer games each year. In total, she and her friends saw 560 soccer games in four years. How many games did they each see in four years? How many games did they each see in one year?

_____

5. Seven buses took 987 people to the World Series. Six buses had an equal number of passengers. An extra bus carried the remaining passengers. How many passengers did the six buses have? How many passengers did the seventh bus have?

_____

You're Out!

Solve the problems and choose the correct path.

START

$5\overline{)720}$ 144   145

$6\overline{)233}$ 38R4   38R5

$9\overline{)874}$ 97R1   97

$3\overline{)168}$ 56   56R1

$7\overline{)763}$ 107   109

$3\overline{)940}$ 314R2   313R1

END

Spaghetti and Meatballs!

The meatballs show the anwers to each problem rounded to the nearest ten thousand. Solve the problems to find whether the answers have been rounded correctly. Write *yes* or *no*.

1. 652 × 80 = 52,160   52,000   no

2. 541 × 63 = _____   30,000   _____

3. 896 × 92 = _____   90,000   _____

4. 724 × 236 = _____   171,000   _____

5. 350 × 672 = _____   240,000   _____

6. 415 × 695 = _____   280,000   _____

7. 756 × 913 = _____   690,000   _____

8. 1,230 × 407 = _____   500,000   _____

Dividing Desserts

Solve the problems. Then color the answer rounded to the nearest hundred.

1. 4)340

2. 3)567

3. 4)972

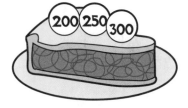

4. 8)3,368

5. 6)4,692

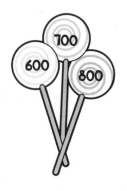

6. 3)9,336

7. 12)948

8. 22)7,150

Which Way?

Write **+**, **−**, **✕**, or **÷** to make each equation true.

1. 1,250 $\boxed{}$ 5 = 250

2. 7,343 $\boxed{}$ 456 = 6,887

3. 45,273 $\boxed{}$ 927 = 46,200

4. 26,568 $\boxed{}$ 19,632 = 46,200

5. 595 $\boxed{}$ 17 = 35

6. 432 $\boxed{}$ 86 = 37,152

7. 1,833 $\boxed{}$ 68 = 124,644

8. 60,047 $\boxed{}$ 27,649 = 87,696

9. 8,943 $\boxed{}$ 3 = 2,981

10. 505,674 $\boxed{}$ 83,218 = 588,892

11. 67,803 $\boxed{}$ 9,624 = 58,179

12. 789,326 $\boxed{}$ 24,562 = 764,764

13. 4,004 $\boxed{}$ 191 = 764,764

14. 7,582 $\boxed{}$ 34 = 223

Driving Days

Solve the problems. You will need to add, subtract, multiply, or divide.

1. Dan drove 4,523 miles in one week. He drove 6,345 miles the next week. How many miles did he drive in all?

_____

2. Paula drove 332 miles every day for a week. How many miles did she drive at the end of the week?

_____

3. Carlos drove 35,672 miles in one year. Rita drove 24,756 miles in one year. How many more miles did Carlos drive than Rita?

_____

4. Mandy bought a car with 50,723 miles on it. She drove it for 43,925 miles before she sold it. How many miles did it have when she sold it?

_____

5. Ahmed drove 728 miles in one week. He drove the same number of miles every day. How many miles did he drive each day?

_____

A Guessing Game

Circle the best estimate.

1. Gumballs
10
100
1,000

2. Paperclips
75
750
7,000

3. Grains of sand
200
2,000
200,000

4. People
30,000
300,000
300,000,000

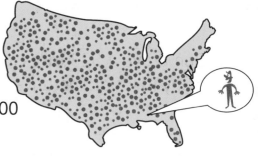

5. Pencils
100
1,000
100,000

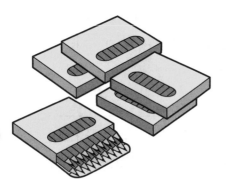

6. Pages
660
1,330
2,600

Percent Practice

Write the decimals and the percents.

1. $\dfrac{50}{100}$ _____ _____

2. $\dfrac{25}{100}$ _____ _____

3. $\dfrac{30}{100}$ _____ _____

4. $\dfrac{75}{100}$ _____ _____

5. $\dfrac{62}{100}$ _____ _____

6. $\dfrac{14}{100}$ _____ _____

7. $\dfrac{89}{100}$ _____ _____

8. $\dfrac{100}{100}$ _____ _____

9. $\dfrac{2}{100}$ _____ _____

10. $\dfrac{98}{100}$ _____ _____

11. $\dfrac{14}{50}$ _____ _____

12. $\dfrac{10}{25}$ _____ _____

13. $\dfrac{2}{20}$ _____ _____

14. $\dfrac{1}{2}$ _____ _____

Practice Makes Perfect

Solve the problems. Some answers may include decimals.

1. 30% of 990 = _____

2. 10% of 50 = _____

3. 50% of 600 = _____

4. 45% of 123 = _____

5. 80% of 756 = _____

6. 75% of 60 = _____

7. 25% of 500 = _____

8. 62% of 621 = _____

9. 94% of 1,000 = _____

10. 33% of 2,000 = _____

11. 26% of 1,349 = _____

12. 57% of 6,320 = _____

13. 4% of 650 = _____

14. 46% of 5,349 = _____

Shopping Spree

Solve the problems.

1. Jenny found a sweater that cost $45. It was on sale for 15% off. How much money did she save? How much did Jenny pay for the sweater?

_____

2. Carl found a jacket that cost $230. It was on sale for 25% off. How much money did he save? How much did Carl pay for the jacket?

_____

3. A store had 80 new CDs for sale. Mario bought 20 of them. What percent of the CDs did he buy?

_____

4. A store had 120 new books. Mrs. Jona bought 35% of them. How many books did she buy?

_____

5. Ben went to the mall yesterday. He took the bus for 14 miles. He walked for 2 miles. What percent of the trip was he on the bus? What percent did he walk?

_____

A Percent Party

Draw a line to match each fraction in the first column with the equivalent amounts in the other columns. The first one is done for you.

1. $\frac{10}{40}$

2. $\frac{15}{30}$

3. $\frac{6}{20}$

4. $\frac{41}{50}$

$\frac{30}{100}$

$\frac{25}{100}$

$\frac{82}{100}$

$\frac{50}{100}$

.25

.82

.50

.30

82%

25%

30%

50%

More or Less

Use the < or > symbol to show which number is greater in each pair.
If the numbers are equal, write =.

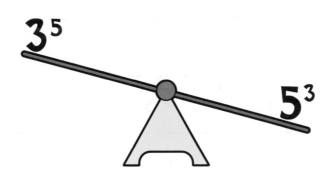

1. 3^5 ☐ 5^3

2. 9^2 ☐ 3^3

3. 4^4 ☐ 16^2

4. 2^6 ☐ 6^2

5. 8^3 ☐ 7^4

6. 6^4 ☐ 9^3

7. 3^7 ☐ 5^4

8. 2^6 ☐ 8^2

9. 5^5 ☐ 9^4

10. 7^3 ☐ 2^8

11. 3^4 ☐ 9^2

12. $4^5 + 2$ ☐ $5^4 + 100$

13. $8^3 - 12$ ☐ $7^3 + 157$

14. 10^5 ☐ 12^4

Why Is It Raining?

Color the prime factorizations of the numbers in the raindrops.
What letter does it make?

$3^2 \times 5$	5^4	11^2	3^9	2^4	$2^4 \times 7$	2^4
7^6	5^2	$5^2 \times 3^2$	$2^3 \times 5$	$2^9 \times 3^3$	$2^3 \times 3$	$3^3 \times 7^3$
$2^4 \times 3^3$	$5^4 \times 2$	$2^2 \times 11$	$5^4 \times 7^3$	$2^2 \times 7$	7^3	3^2
2^2	$5^2 \times 3^3$	3^2	$2^2 \times 3^2$	$2^6 \times 3^2$	2^3	$2^4 \times 3^3$
$3^4 \times 2$	$2^3 \times 3^3$	7^5	$2^2 \times 3$	11^4	5^6	$2^5 \times 3$
3^6	5^7	$7^4 \times 3^3$	2^5	7^3	$2^8 \times 3^2$	3^9
$2^3 \times 3^5$	$2^6 \times 3^2$	7^2	2×5^2	$2^4 \times 3$	11^3	2^3

25 44 12 36 45
32 24 16 50
28

The letter _____

A Perfect Fit

Write the numbers on the lines from least to greatest.
Then order the numbers on the dolls.

$1\frac{3}{4}$ .34   0   1 $\frac{1}{2}$ $1\frac{1}{2}$ $\frac{75}{100}$ 1.66

___ ___ ___ ___ ___ ___ ___ ___

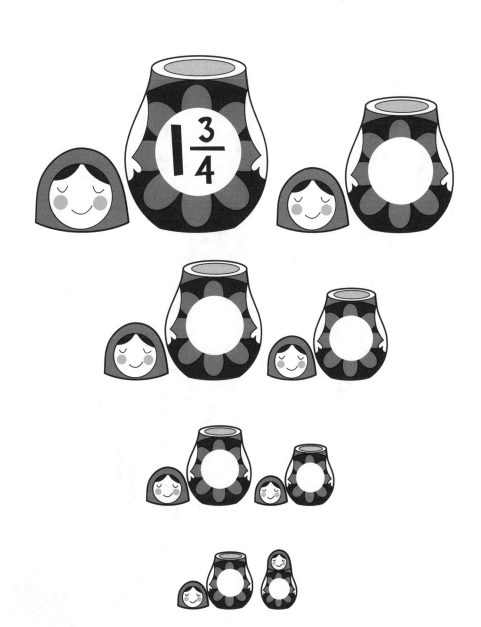

Decimal Daze

Solve the problems.

1.   1.34
    + 2.69

2.   3.56
    + 7.89

3.   10.72
    + 33.45

4.   45.89
    + 66.91

5.   101.34
    + 344.56

6.   4.024
    + 8.564

7.   3.223
    + 8.909

8.   4.578
    + 5.614

9.   12.343
    + 76.657

10.   102.445
    + 465.003

11.   9.034
    + 5.06

12.   13.56
    + 56.8

13.   605.50
    + 15.83

14.   14.123
    + 19.38

1.34+2.69 =?

Dreaming about Decimals

Solve the problems.

1. 5.8
   − 4.2
   _____

2. 8.76
   − 5.03
   _____

3. 20.65
   − 18.14
   _____

4. 34.59
   − 29.27
   _____

5. 7.4
   − 5.9
   _____

6. 15.6
   − 13.7
   _____

7. 304.1
   − 243.5
   _____

8. 42.56
   − 35.67
   _____

9. 27.83
   − 14.05
   _____

10. 34.56
   − 4.99
   _____

11. 202.44
   − 169.54
   _____

12. 5.768
   − 3.124
   _____

13. 23.459
   − 12.862
   _____

14. 35.704
   − 21.98
   _____

5.8−4.2 =?

Bike-A-Thon

Four students biked to raise money. Add or subtract to solve the problems.

	Miles on Monday	Miles on Tuesday
Diana	42.25	13.45
Ricardo	50.34	16.76
Wendy	26.33	27.49
David	32.97	21.06

1. How many more miles did Diana bike on Monday than on Tuesday?

_____

2. How many miles did Wendy bike altogether?

_____

3. How many more miles did David bike than Wendy on Monday?

_____

4. How many more miles did Ricardo bike than Diana on Tuesday?

_____

5. Who biked the most miles altogether? Who biked the least?

_____

Solve the problems. Use the chart on page 32.
Multiply and round to the nearest hundredth.

6. Wendy's mom pledged to pay $1.25 for every mile Wendy biked. How much money did Wendy make on Monday?

_____

7. David's brother pledged to pay 50¢ for every mile he biked. How much money did David make on Tuesday?

_____

8. Ricardo's friend pledged 32¢ for every mile he biked. How much money did Ricardo make on Monday?

_____

9. Diana's dad pledged $1.46 for every mile she biked. How much money did she make on Monday?

_____

10. How much money did Diana make on Tuesday?

_____

Decimal Division

Solve the problems. Write the answers in decimals.

1. $.5\overline{)65}$

2. $.3\overline{)9}$

3. $.9\overline{)18}$

4. $2\overline{)1.5}$

5. $2\overline{)5.6}$

6. $5\overline{)2.8}$

7. $4\overline{)10.3}$

8. $7\overline{)8.89}$

9. $3\overline{)32.49}$

10. $5\overline{)127.95}$

11. $10\overline{)34.56}$

12. $12\overline{)144.6}$

13. $.1\overline{)23.06}$

14. $.2\overline{)5.7}$

Movie Mania

Solve the problems. Multiply or divide. Round answers to the nearest hundredth.

1. Rick goes to the movies with six friends. They are all students. How much is the total price for the tickets?

   _____

2. Rick and two of his friends share a large popcorn and a large soda. They divide the cost evenly. How much do they each have to pay?

   _____

3. Rick's parents go to the movie. They buy tickets for themselves and for Rick's grandmother. They divide the price evenly between the two of them. How much do they each pay?

   _____

4. Janet and three friends get two large popcorns and four small sodas. They split the price. How much do they each pay?

   _____

5. Rick's aunt, uncle, and six cousins go to the movie, too. The cousins are all students. How much does it cost for them to go to the movie?

   _____

The Missing Mitten

Help Carlos find his mitten. Choose the operation to follow the correct path.

$2.34 \;\square\; 10.29 = 12.63$

$15.9 \;\square\; 3 = 5.3$ ÷

$28.44 \;\square\; 2.4 = 11.85$

$6.91 \;\square\; 5.86 = 1.05$

$12.2 \;\square\; .35 = 4.27$

$43.12 \;\square\; .75 = 32.34$

$53.02 \;\square\; 5.74 = 47.28$

$121.03 \;\square\; 66.7 = 187.73$ +

START

END

Picture It!

Solve the problems.

1. 12 + (–11) = _____

2. 34 + (–42) = _____

3. (–21) + 19 = _____

4. 56 + (–76) = _____

5. (–48) + 24 = _____

6. (–19) + 45 = _____

7. 72 + (–103) = _____

8. 123 + (–66) = _____

9. 402 + (–500) = _____

10. (–220) + 50 = _____

11. (–345) + 603 = _____

12. 324 + (–42) = _____

13. 900 + (–1,000) = _____

14. (–25) + 25 = _____

Snapshot Subtraction

Solve the problems.

1. (−6) − 2 = _____

2. (−18) − 14 = _____

3. (−33) − 47 = _____

4. (−52) − 75 = _____

5. (−43) − 43 = _____

6. (−59) − 16 = _____

7. (−98) − 82 = _____

8. (−45) − 0 = _____

9. (−270) − 27 = _____

10. (−324) − 1 = _____

11. (−606) − 127 = _____

12. (−250) − 33 = _____

13. (−409) − 120 = _____

14. (−525) − 175 = _____

Picture Perfect Problems

Solve the problems.

1. 16 + (– 5) = _____

2. (–60) – 26 = _____

3. (–41) – 16 = _____

4. (–32) + 65 = _____

5. 123 + (– 92) = _____

6. 302 + (–411) = _____

7. (–59) – 36 = _____

8. (–150) + 76 = _____

9. 259 + (–300) = _____

10. (–25) – 20 = _____

11. (–126) – 127 = _____

12. 755 + (–301) = _____

13. (–503) – 286 = _____

14. (–285) + 531 = _____

Fraction Frenzy

Solve the problems. Write the answers in the simplest form.

1. $\dfrac{1}{2} + \dfrac{1}{2} =$ _____

2. $\dfrac{1}{8} + \dfrac{3}{8} =$ _____

3. $\dfrac{2}{20} + \dfrac{12}{20} =$ _____

4. $\dfrac{1}{2} + \dfrac{1}{4} =$ _____

5. $\dfrac{1}{8} + \dfrac{2}{4} =$ _____

6. $\dfrac{2}{6} + \dfrac{3}{6} =$ _____

7. $\dfrac{2}{12} + \dfrac{6}{12} =$ _____

8. $\dfrac{2}{4} + \dfrac{3}{8} =$ _____

9. $\dfrac{1}{3} + \dfrac{2}{6} =$ _____

10. $\dfrac{3}{5} + \dfrac{2}{10} =$ _____

11. $\dfrac{2}{6} + \dfrac{1}{2} =$ _____

12. $\dfrac{1}{9} + \dfrac{2}{3} =$ _____

13. $\dfrac{3}{4} + \dfrac{1}{6} =$ _____

14. $\dfrac{1}{5} + \dfrac{4}{10} =$ _____

Floating in Fractions

Solve the problems. Write the answers in the simplest form.

1. $\dfrac{2}{3} - \dfrac{1}{3} =$ _____

2. $\dfrac{4}{5} - \dfrac{2}{5} =$ _____

3. $\dfrac{6}{10} - \dfrac{3}{10} =$ _____

4. $\dfrac{4}{6} - \dfrac{1}{6} =$ _____

5. $\dfrac{10}{15} - \dfrac{5}{15} =$ _____

6. $\dfrac{6}{7} - \dfrac{3}{7} =$ _____

7. $\dfrac{6}{12} - \dfrac{1}{6} =$ _____

8. $\dfrac{2}{3} - \dfrac{1}{2} =$ _____

9. $\dfrac{3}{4} - \dfrac{1}{2} =$ _____

10. $\dfrac{3}{5} - \dfrac{1}{10} =$ _____

11. $\dfrac{4}{6} - \dfrac{2}{3} =$ _____

12. $\dfrac{5}{8} - \dfrac{2}{4} =$ _____

13. $\dfrac{3}{4} - \dfrac{3}{12} =$ _____

14. $\dfrac{4}{5} - \dfrac{1}{15} =$ _____

A Good Catch!

Solve the problems. Then color the correct answer.
Sometimes more than one answer is possible.

1.
$$\frac{6}{8} + \frac{1}{8} =$$

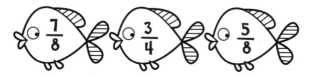

$\frac{7}{8}$ · $\frac{3}{4}$ · $\frac{5}{8}$

2.
$$\frac{3}{4} - \frac{1}{4} =$$

$\frac{2}{4}$ · $\frac{1}{2}$ · 1

3.
$$\frac{7}{10} - \frac{2}{10} =$$

$\frac{9}{10}$ · $\frac{5}{10}$ · $\frac{1}{2}$

4.
$$\frac{2}{18} + \frac{4}{18} =$$

$\frac{6}{18}$ · $\frac{3}{9}$ · $\frac{1}{3}$

5.
$$\frac{3}{4} - \frac{2}{3} =$$

$\frac{2}{6}$ · $\frac{1}{12}$ · $\frac{1}{2}$

6.
$$\frac{4}{5} + \frac{2}{10} =$$

$\frac{10}{10}$ · $\frac{6}{10}$ · 1

7.
$$\frac{2}{6} + \frac{1}{3} =$$

$\frac{2}{3}$ · $\frac{4}{6}$ · 0

8.
$$\frac{9}{10} - \frac{3}{5} =$$

$\frac{1}{2}$ · $\frac{3}{10}$ · $\frac{6}{10}$

Crazy Cooks

Solve the problems. Write the answers in the simplest form.

1. Maria is making cookies. She needs to stir in $1\frac{1}{2}$ cups of flour with other dry ingredients. After she adds the wet ingredients, she needs to stir in another $\frac{1}{2}$ cup of flour. How much flour does she need altogether?

_____

2. Paul is making a cake. He drops $1\frac{3}{4}$ cups of sugar on the floor. Then he drops another $\frac{1}{2}$ cup of sugar on the floor. How much sugar does he drop altogether?

_____

3. Maria gives her cookies to her family. Her dad eats $4\frac{1}{2}$ cookies in the morning. He eats 5 cookies in the afternoon, and he eats $2\frac{3}{4}$ cookies at night. How many cookies does he eat in all?

_____

4. Paul's family eats his cake. His mom eats $1\frac{1}{2}$ pieces. His sister eats $\frac{1}{2}$ piece. His father eats $1\frac{2}{3}$ pieces. He eats 2 pieces. How many pieces are eaten in all?

_____

5. It takes Maria $2\frac{5}{8}$ of an hour to make her cookies. It takes Paul $3\frac{1}{4}$ hours to make his cake. How much time do they spend cooking in all?

_____

Pizza Party

Solve the problems. Write the answers in the simplest form.

1. Jack ate $1\frac{3}{4}$ pizzas. Lee ate $1\frac{2}{3}$ pizzas. How much more pizza did Jack eat than Lee?

_____

2. Carla ate $1\frac{1}{2}$ pizzas. Mandy ate $2\frac{5}{6}$ pizzas. How much more pizza did Mandy eat than Carla?

_____

3. Carla ate $3\frac{3}{4}$ breadsticks. Jack ate $4\frac{1}{8}$ breadsticks. How many more breadsticks did Jack eat than Carla?

_____

4. Lee ate $3\frac{1}{3}$ breadsticks. Mandy ate $1\frac{1}{2}$ breadsticks. How many more breadsticks did Lee eat than Mandy?

_____

5. Carla drank $3\frac{3}{4}$ sodas. Lee drank $1\frac{1}{3}$ sodas. How many more sodas did Carla drink than Lee?

_____

A Bad Breakfast

Solve the problems. Then write the letter that matches the answer to find out what Bill had for breakfast. The first one is done for you.

C	I	E	K	O	S	X
$1\frac{1}{4}$	$1\frac{3}{4}$	2	$1\frac{1}{2}$	3	$4\frac{1}{4}$	$5\frac{3}{4}$

What did Bill have for breakfast?

$\underline{\quad S \quad}$

$1\frac{3}{4} + 2\frac{2}{4}$

$\frac{7}{4} + \frac{10}{4}$

$\frac{17}{4} = 4\frac{1}{4}$

$\underline{\qquad}$

$2\frac{1}{8} - \frac{3}{8}$

$\underline{\qquad}$

$3\frac{1}{2} + 2\frac{1}{4}$

$\underline{\qquad}$ $\underline{\qquad}$ $\underline{\qquad}$ $\underline{\qquad}$ $\underline{\qquad}$ $\underline{\qquad}$ $\underline{\qquad}$!

$2\frac{1}{2} - 1\frac{1}{4}$ $1\frac{1}{6} + 1\frac{10}{12}$ $5\frac{1}{2} - 2\frac{2}{4}$ $4\frac{1}{6} - 2\frac{2}{3}$ $1\frac{1}{2} + \frac{1}{4}$ $1\frac{7}{8} + \frac{2}{16}$ $7 - 2\frac{3}{4}$

Fraction Safari

Solve the problems. Write the answers in the simplest form.

1. $\frac{1}{4} \times \frac{1}{2} = $ _____

2. $\frac{3}{4} \times \frac{2}{3} = $ _____

3. $\frac{2}{5} \times \frac{1}{2} = $ _____

4. $\frac{1}{3} \times \frac{3}{4} = $ _____

5. $\frac{9}{10} \times 3 = $ _____

6. $\frac{1}{4} \times 4 = $ _____

7. $1\frac{1}{2} \times 2 = $ _____

8. $2\frac{2}{3} \times 3 = $ _____

9. $1\frac{1}{4} \times 5 = $ _____

10. $1\frac{1}{2} \times \frac{1}{2} = $ _____

11. $2\frac{1}{3} \times 1\frac{2}{3} = $ _____

12. $1\frac{4}{5} \times 2\frac{1}{2} = $ _____

13. $3\frac{1}{4} \times 1\frac{1}{2} = $ _____

14. $1\frac{2}{3} \times 2\frac{1}{4} = $ _____

Looking for Lions

Solve the problems. Write the answers in the simplest form.

1. $\dfrac{3}{4} \div \dfrac{1}{4} =$ _____

2. $\dfrac{4}{5} \div \dfrac{2}{5} =$ _____

3. $\dfrac{1}{4} \div \dfrac{1}{4} =$ _____

4. $\dfrac{2}{3} \div \dfrac{1}{3} =$ _____

5. $\dfrac{1}{2} \div \dfrac{1}{3} =$ _____

6. $\dfrac{3}{4} \div \dfrac{1}{8} =$ _____

7. $\dfrac{7}{8} \div \dfrac{3}{4} =$ _____

8. $\dfrac{2}{5} \div \dfrac{1}{3} =$ _____

9. $4 \div \dfrac{3}{4} =$ _____

10. $9 \div \dfrac{1}{2} =$ _____

11. $1\dfrac{1}{2} \div \dfrac{3}{4} =$ _____

12. $2\dfrac{1}{3} \div 1\dfrac{2}{3} =$ _____

13. $5\dfrac{1}{4} \div 1\dfrac{3}{4} =$ _____

14. $3\dfrac{1}{3} \div 1\dfrac{1}{2} =$ _____

Fraction Find

Solve the problems. Then draw a line to the matching numbers.

1. 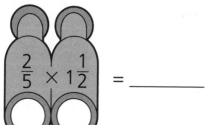 $\frac{2}{5} \times 1\frac{1}{2}$ = _____

$2\frac{2}{5}$

2. 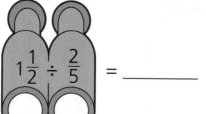 $1\frac{1}{2} \div \frac{2}{5}$ = _____

$3\frac{3}{4}$

3. 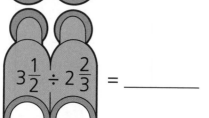 $3\frac{1}{2} \div 2\frac{2}{3}$ = _____

6

4. 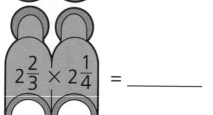 $2\frac{2}{3} \times 2\frac{1}{4}$ = _____

$6\frac{1}{2}$

5. 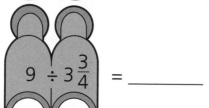 $9 \div 3\frac{3}{4}$ = _____

$\frac{3}{5}$

6. 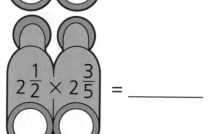 $2\frac{1}{2} \times 2\frac{3}{5}$ = _____

$1\frac{5}{16}$

Paint Problems

Solve the problems.

1. It takes $\frac{3}{4}$ a can of paint to paint one wall in Julia's kitchen. She's going to paint 4 walls. How many cans of paint does she need?

_____

2. It takes $4\frac{2}{3}$ cans of paint to paint one room in Doug's house. He's going to paint 5 rooms. How many cans of paint does he need?

_____

3. It takes $1\frac{1}{2}$ cans of paint to paint one wall in Belinda's bedroom. She's going to paint $2\frac{1}{2}$ walls. How many cans of paint does she need?

_____

4. It takes Pablo $1\frac{3}{4}$ hours to paint one wall. He paints $3\frac{1}{2}$ walls. How long does it take him?

_____

5. It takes Jenny $5\frac{1}{3}$ hours to paint one room. She paints 2 rooms. How long does it take her?

_____

Fix it!

Solve the problems.

1. George fixes 3 drawers in his desk. It takes him $1\frac{1}{2}$ hours to fix the drawers. It takes him an equal amount of time to fix each drawer. How long does it take him to fix each drawer?

_____

2. Nicole needs $5\frac{3}{4}$ pieces of wood to make two equal shelves. How many pieces of wood does she need for each shelf?

_____

3. Miguel and his two friends paint $6\frac{1}{4}$ walls on Sunday. They each paint the same number of walls. How many walls do they each paint?

_____

4. Victoria uses $3\frac{3}{4}$ cans of paint to paint $2\frac{1}{2}$ walls. She uses the same amount of paint on each wall. How much paint does she use on each wall?

_____

5. Jin builds 6 shelves on Tuesday. It takes him $2\frac{1}{2}$ hours. It takes him the same amount of time to build each shelf. How long does it take him to build each shelf?

_____

House Help

Solve the problems. Then color the answers below to find out how many houses Mr. Smyth and Linda painted.

1. $\frac{3}{4} \times \frac{2}{3} =$ _____

2. $\frac{2}{4} \div \frac{2}{3} =$ _____

3. $2 \times 1\frac{1}{4} =$ _____

4. $5 \times \frac{3}{4} =$ _____

5. $\frac{2}{5} \div \frac{1}{2} =$ _____

6. $4 \div \frac{1}{4} =$ _____

7. $1\frac{1}{2} \times 3\frac{1}{2} =$ _____

8. $3\frac{1}{4} \times 2\frac{1}{2} =$ _____

9. $1\frac{2}{3} \div 1\frac{1}{2} =$ _____

10. $1\frac{3}{4} \div 1\frac{1}{6} =$ _____

$1\frac{3}{4}$	$\frac{3}{4}$	$4\frac{3}{4}$	$5\frac{1}{4}$	$16\frac{3}{4}$
$\frac{2}{9}$	$1\frac{1}{9}$	4	$3\frac{3}{4}$	$2\frac{2}{5}$
13	16	$\frac{1}{2}$	$8\frac{1}{8}$	$\frac{1}{3}$
$5\frac{1}{2}$	7	$3\frac{1}{4}$	$1\frac{1}{2}$	9
$\frac{3}{5}$	$\frac{1}{4}$	$2\frac{2}{3}$	$2\frac{1}{2}$	$2\frac{4}{10}$
3	$16\frac{1}{2}$	5	$\frac{4}{5}$	17

Sewing Spree

Solve the problems.

1. Mrs. Roosevelt is making curtains. She has $10\frac{1}{2}$ yards of fabric. Each curtain uses $2\frac{1}{4}$ yards of fabric. How many curtains can she make? Round to the nearest whole number.

_____

2. How many yards of fabric does Mrs. Roosevelt have left over?

_____

3. Cameron is making 4 shirts. She needs $1\frac{2}{3}$ yards of fabric for each shirt. How much fabric does she need?

_____

4. Cameron bought $8\frac{1}{2}$ yards of fabric. How much does she have left over?

_____

5. John bought $1\frac{1}{2}$ yards of purple fabric, $2\frac{2}{3}$ yards of red fabric, and $5\frac{1}{4}$ yards of green fabric. How much fabric does he have altogether?

_____

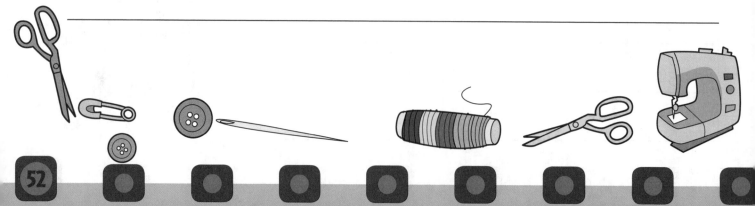

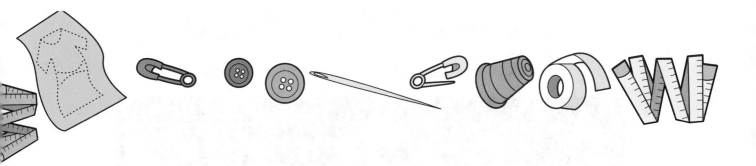

6. It took Penny $1\frac{1}{2}$ hours to make 3 skirts. It took her an equal amount of time to make each skirt. How long did it take her to make each skirt?

_____

7. Penny needed $2\frac{1}{3}$ yards of fabric for each skirt. How many yards did she need altogether?

_____

8. Mr. Jackson made curtains that were $1\frac{1}{2}$ feet too long. The curtains were $6\frac{3}{4}$ feet long. How long should the curtains be?

_____

9. Todd bought $3\frac{3}{4}$ yards of fabric. Lilly bought $2\frac{1}{2}$ yards of fabric. Donna bought $3\frac{1}{8}$ yards of fabric. How much fabric did they buy altogether?

_____

10. Todd, Lilly, and Donna made a curtain for the theater with their fabric. They used $9\frac{3}{8}$ yards of fabric. How much fabric did they have left over?

_____

Moon Over Math

Look at the graph and answer the questions.

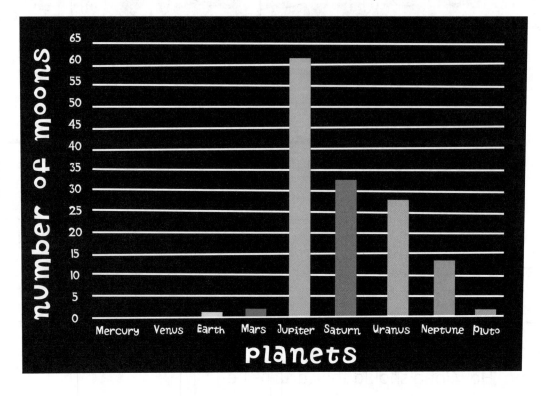

1. Which planet has the most moons? How many moons does it have?

_____

2. How many moons does Pluto have?

_____

3. How many more moons does Saturn have than Neptune?

_____

4. How many more moons does Uranus have than Mars?

_____

5. What is the total number of moons in the solar system?

_____

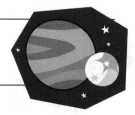

Weigh to Go!

If you weigh 100 pounds on Earth, this graph shows what you would weigh on some of the other planets. Numbers are rounded to the nearest ten. Look at the graph and answer the questions.

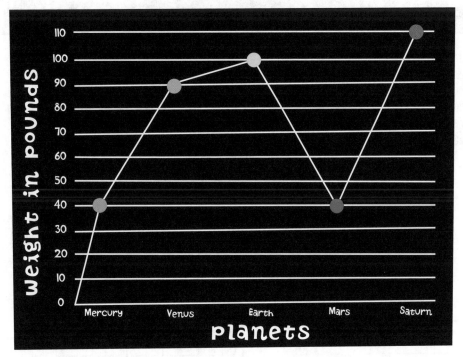

1. Lisa weighs 100 pounds on Earth. What does she weigh on Saturn?

_____

2. Jim weighs 150 pounds on Earth. What does he weigh on Mars?

_____

3. Luke weighs 40 pounds on Mars. Kent weighs 100 pounds on Venus. Who weighs more on Earth?

_____

4. Luke has two dogs. Scruffy weighs 20 pounds on Mercury. Rocky weighs 11 pounds on Saturn. Which dog weighs less on Earth?

_____

5. Three boxes weigh 30 pounds each on Venus. What do they weigh in all on Venus? What do they weigh in all on Earth?

_____

Great Grids

Match the grids to their titles. Then write the coordinates for the objects given. The first one is done for you.

Baseball Positions	My Neighborhood	A Museum Plan

1. _____

airplane ___(5, 5)___

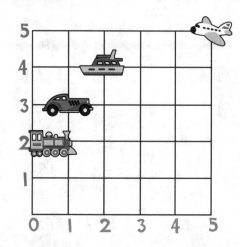

2. _____

batter _____

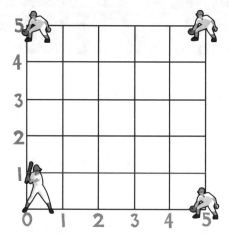

3. _____

bank _____

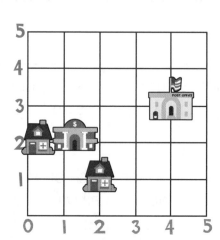

Neighborhood Numbers

Matt put important places in his neighborhood on a grid. Write the coordinates for the places. The first one is done for you.

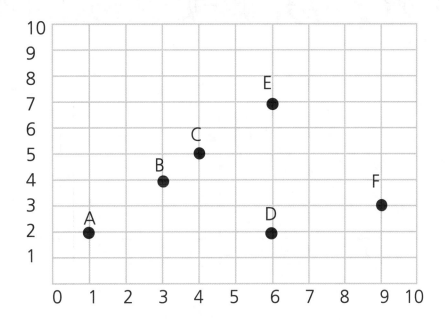

Place	Letter	Ordered Pair
1. His house	A	(1, 2)
2. The library	B	_____
3. The post office	C	_____
4. His school	D	_____
5. The park	E	_____
6. The bank	F	_____

Coordinated Order

Graph and label the ordered pairs on the grid.

A (0, 3)	B (1, 5)	C (–2, 4)	D (–3, 5)	E (5, –1)
F (–5, 3)	G (–3, –4)	H (2, –4)	I (0, –4)	J (–3, –2)

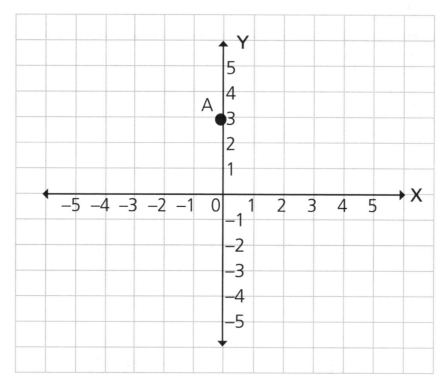

I'D LIKE A (0,3) AND A (–3,5)

MENU

A Surprise Sighting

Graph the ordered pairs in the box on the grid. Connect the points as you go to find out what Susie sees.

(2, 0) (4, –3) (0, –1) (–4, –3) (–2, 0) (–4, 3) (–1, 1) (0, 3) (1, 1) (4, 3)

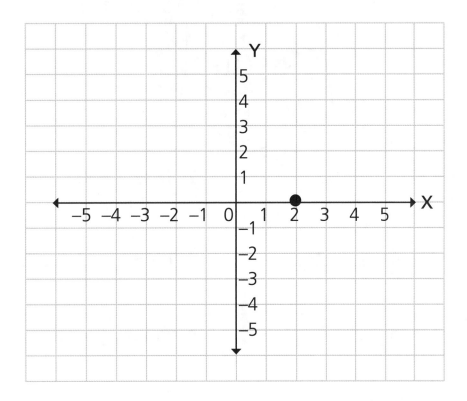

Susie sees a _____.

Lost and Found

Find the value for the letter that will make each equation true.

1. $3n + 2 = 17$ _____

2. $5a + 11 = 31$ _____

3. $8 + a + 27 = 44$ _____

4. $12y - 4 = 20$ _____

5. $120 \div 2p = 30$ _____

6. $70 + 2 - y = 22$ _____

7. $4n + (-8) = 12$ _____

8. $(6 \times 3) \div b = 6$ _____

9. $200 + 6 - x = 113$ _____

10. $4n \times 5 = 120$ _____

11. $7a \div 8 = 7$ _____

12. $(18 \div 2) \times b = 108$ _____

13. $203 + y = 157$ _____

14. $(9x \div 3) + 2 = 29$ _____

Block Buster

Write an equation and then solve the problem. The first one is done for you.

> b = unknown blocks
> d = unknown days
> m = unknown minute

1. Julia walks her dog 14 blocks a day. She walked her dog for *n* days. If she walks for a total of 70 blocks in one week, how many days did she walk her dog?

$14d = 70 \quad d = 5$

2. Raul lives 5 blocks north of John. Raul lives 20 blocks north of north of Dina. How many blocks north of Dina does John live?

_____

3. It takes Leo 60 minutes to get to school. He walks for 20 minutes. He takes the bus for the rest of the time. How long is he on the bus?

_____

4. Jennifer walked 5 blocks on Sunday. On Monday through Saturday she walked the same amount of blocks each day. At the end of the week, she walked 53 blocks. How many blocks did she walk each day Monday through Saturday?

_____

5. Carla went to the video store. She walked for 14 blocks. She noticed she dropped her scarf. She walked back 2 blocks. The video store is 24 blocks from her house. How many blocks did she walk after she dropped her scarf?

_____

Diego's Day

Substitute the numbers for the variables. Are the problems correct? Circle the letters for the correct problems. Cross out the letters for the wrong problems. Then see what it spells to see where Diego went. The first one is done for you.

a	b	k	n	p	t	r	x
76	15	7	−9	10	6	12	5

1.
$$\textcircled{p}$$

$2p + 20 = 40$

2.
$$t$$

$5t \div 2 = 13$

3.
$$a$$

$203 + a + 127 = 406$

4.
$$k$$

$8k + 5 = 60$

5.
$$x$$

$(7 \times 5) \div x = 4$

6.
$$r$$

$9r \div (3 \times 2) = 18$

7.
$$b$$

$7 + b + (-15) = 0$

8.
$$n$$

$23 + n = 32$

9.
$$k$$

$(25 + 38) \div k = 9$

10.
$$a$$

$(38 \times 2) \div a = 11$

Diego went to the _____.

Which Comes First?

Solve the problems.

1. 8(4 + 2) = _____

2. 5(13 + 7) = _____

3. 22(9 + 2) = _____

4. 6(23 + 10) = _____

5. 15(9 + 3) = _____

6. 121(7 + 6) = _____

7. 9(42 + 2) = _____

8. 3(8 + 11) = _____

9. 4(9 + 9) = _____

10. 10(120 + 45) = _____

11. 7(16 + 2) = _____

12. 9(15 + 15) = _____

13. 7(1 + 3 + 2) = _____

14. 2(5 + 7 + 8) = _____

Chickens and Chickadees

Draw a line to match each problem in the first column with the equivalent amounts in the other columns. The first one is done for you.

1. 8
   × 15

   (8 × 30) + (8 × 7)

   180 + 42

   222

2. 6
   × 37

   (6 × 30) + (6 × 7)

   40 + 20

   296

3. 4
   × 15

   (8 × 10) + (8 × 5)

   240 + 56

   60

4. 8
   × 37

   (4 × 10) + (4 × 5)

   80 + 40

   120

Cracking the Code

Solve for *n*.

1. 9 × 19 = (9 × 10) + (9 × *n*)

_____

2. 6 × 14 = (6 × *n*) + (6 × 4)

_____

3. 5 × 53 = (5 × 50) + (5 × *n*)

_____

4. 11 × 72 = (11 × 70) + (11 × *n*)

_____

5. 8 × 114 = (8 × *n*) + (8 × 14)

_____

6. 3 × 87 = (3 × 80) + (3 × *n*)

_____

7. *n* × 23 = (7 × 20) + (7 × 3)

_____

8. 4 × *n* = (4 × 10) + (4 × 6)

_____

9. 9 × 42 = (*n* × 40) + (*n* × 2)

_____

10. 12 × 13 = (12 × 10) + (12 × *n*)

_____

11. 5 × *n* = (5 × 100) + (5 × 6)

_____

12. *n* × 54 = (8 × 50) + (8 × 4)

_____

13. 6 × *n* = (6 × 60) + (6 × 7)

_____

14. 50 × 24 = (50 × *n*) + (50 × 4)

_____

Equestrian Equations

Circle the equation that makes every ordered pair in the table true.
Then graph the ordered pairs.

1.

x	y
–4	6
–1	3
0	2
2	0
5	–3

$x + y = 2$

$2x + y = 1$

$x = y \times 0$

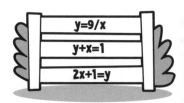

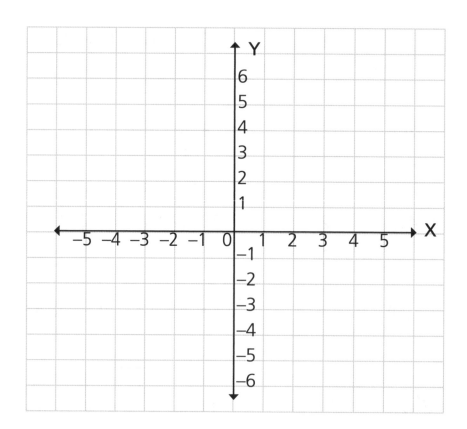

2.

x	y
−3	−5
−1	−1
0	1
1	3
2	5

$y = 9 / x$

$y + x = 1$

$2x + 1 = y$

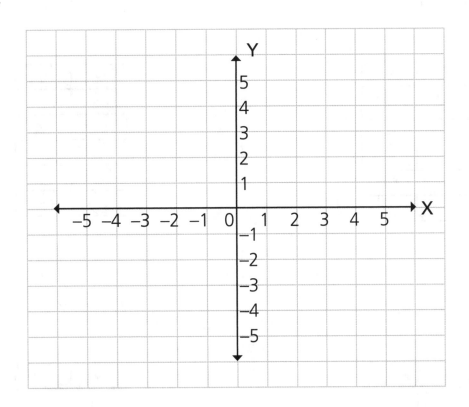

Missing in Action

Complete the charts. The first part of the first one is done for you.

1. $4x + 5 = y$

x	y
−2	−3
	1
0	
1	
	17

2. $x = 3y \div 2$

x	y
−9	
	−4
	2
6	
	6

3. $2x + 2 = y$

x	y
−5	
	−4
0	
	6
12	

4. $7x = y$

x	y
−4	
	−14
	7
4	
	70

Sandra Sleuth

Color the ordered pairs that work in the equation to find out where Sandra will find a treasure.

$$4x + 5 = y$$

(–1, 1)	(0, 6)	(0, 0)	(2, –13)	(–3, –7)
(–5, 15)	(0, 5)	(1, –9)	(2, 13)	(3, 7)
(–6, –20)	(7, 31)	(–4, –11)	(3, –7)	(–9, 30)
(–2, 3)	(3, 17)	(2, 20)	(–10, –35)	(9, 1)
(5, 25)	(1, 1)	(4, 17)	(5, 0)	(1, 9)

_____ marks the spot where Sandra will find the treasure.

Perimeter Practice

Find the perimeter of each shape.

1. _____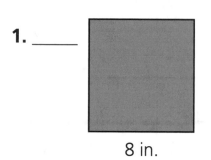

8 in.

2. _____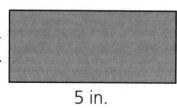

9 in.

5 in.

3. _____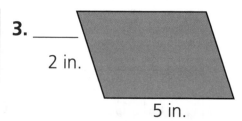

2 in.

5 in.

4. _____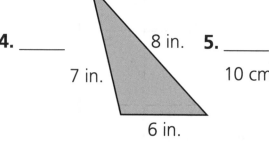

8 in.

7 in.

6 in.

5. _____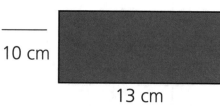

10 cm

13 cm

6. _____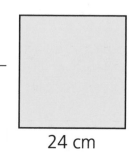

24 cm

7. _____

14 cm

10 cm

8. _____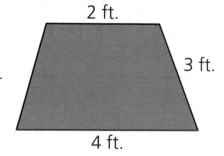

2 ft.

3 ft.

4 ft.

9. _____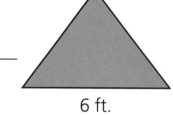

6 ft.

Shape Up!

Color the shapes that have a perimeter of 124 inches.

1.

29 in.

2.

18 in.

44 in.

3.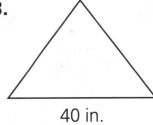

40 in.

4.

31 in.

5.

24 in

38 in.

6.

32 in.

40 in.

7.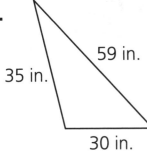

35 in.

59 in.

30 in.

8.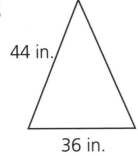

44 in.

36 in.

9.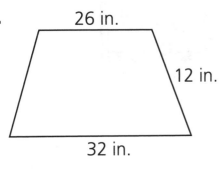

26 in.

12 in.

32 in.

All About Area

Find the area of the following shapes. Then write <, >, or =.

1.

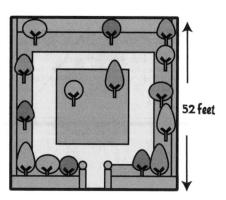

A = _____

☐

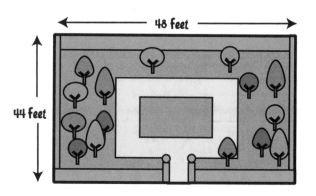

A = _____

2.

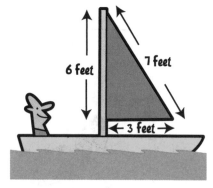

A = _____

☐

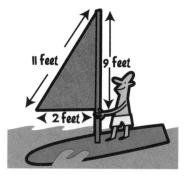

A = _____

3.

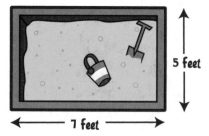

A = _____

☐

A = _____

4.

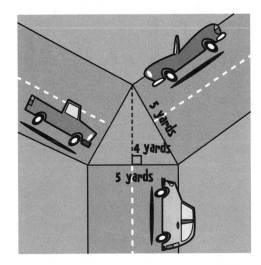

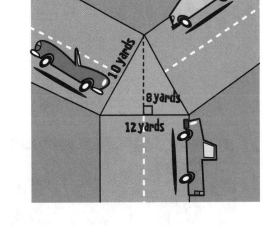

A = _____

A = _____

5.

22 feet

110 feet

20 feet

121 feet

A = _____

A = _____

6.

4 feet

8.5 feet

3.5 feet

9 feet

A = _____

A = _____

A Room for Rufus, A Place for Peanut

Find the volume of each object.

1.

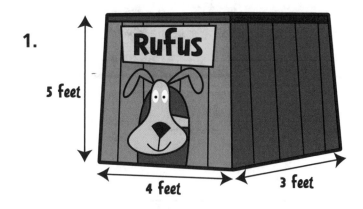

5 feet

4 feet   3 feet

Volume = _____

2. 10 inches

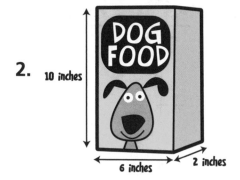

6 inches   2 inches

Volume = _____

3.

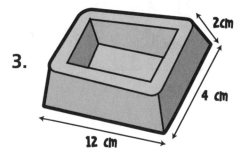

2cm

4 cm

12 cm

Volume = _____

4.

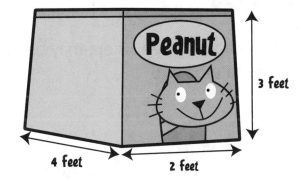

3 feet

4 feet

2 feet

Volume = _____

5.

5 inches

CAT FOOD

4 inches   3 inches

Volume = _____

6.

2 feet   2 feet

4 feet

Volume = _____

Birthday Bash

Color the objects that have the same volume as the amount given. There may be more than one correct answer for each problem.

1. 672 inches³

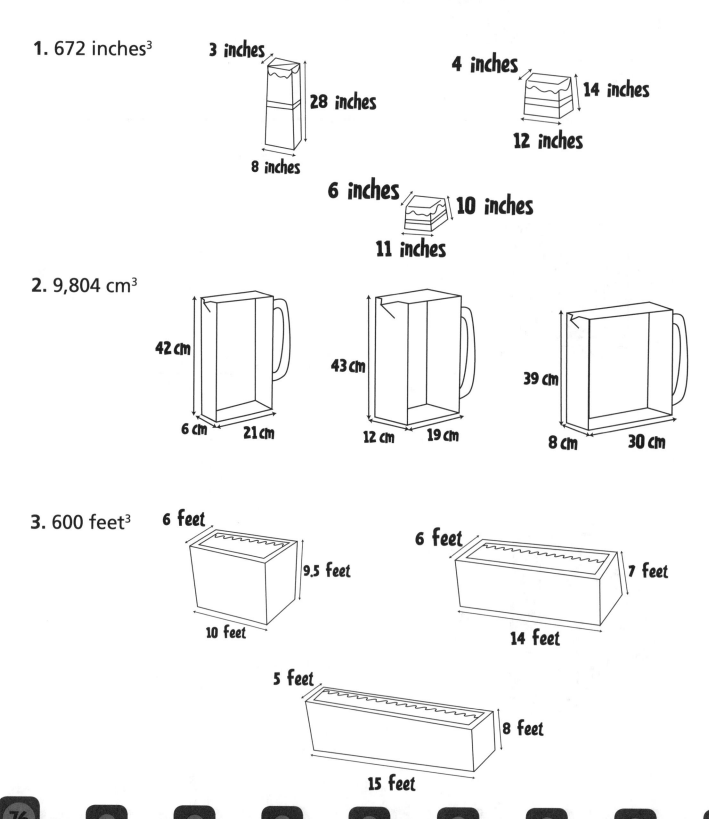

3 inches

28 inches

8 inches

4 inches

14 inches

12 inches

6 inches

10 inches

11 inches

2. 9,804 cm³

42 cm

6 cm   21 cm

43 cm

12 cm   19 cm

39 cm

8 cm   30 cm

3. 600 feet³

6 feet

9.5 feet

10 feet

6 feet

7 feet

14 feet

5 feet

8 feet

15 feet

Perimeter Problems

Solve the problems.

1. Dan walks around the outside of the pool. How far does he walk?

_____

2. Mr. Freemont wants to buy a cover for the pool. What is the area of the cover that he needs?

_____

3. Mrs. Freemont wants to fill the pool with water. How much space will she need to fill?

_____

4. Nancy walks around the pool three times. How far does she walk?

_____

5. Mr. Freemont buys a cover that has an area of 120 ft^2. How many square feet too small is it?

_____

Cake and Candles

Round the number and choose the correct path.

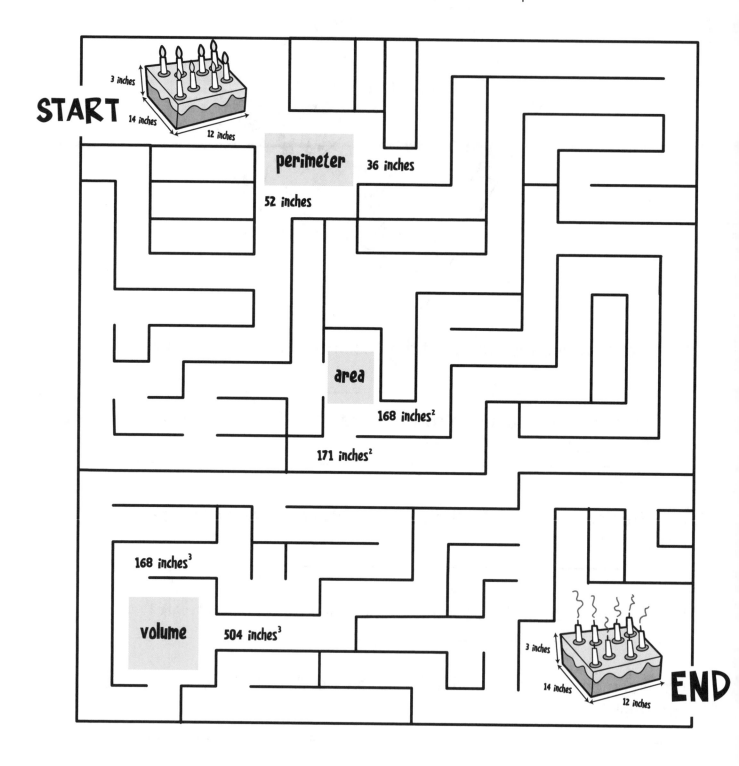

START

3 inches
14 inches
12 inches

perimeter   36 inches

52 inches

area

168 inches²

171 inches²

168 inches³

volume   504 inches³

3 inches
14 inches
12 inches

END

Andrea the Architect

Read and draw. You will need a ruler.

1. Draw a line that is 12 centimeters long.

2. Draw a line that is 6 centimeters long.

3. Draw a line that is 3 centimeters long.

4. Draw two parallel lines that are each 9 centimeters long.

5. Draw two perpendicular lines that are each 13 centimeters long.

Angie's Angles

Measure the angles. You will need a protractor. Then write the angle and circle the type of angle.

1. 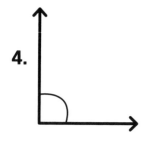 _____ right   obtuse   acute

2. 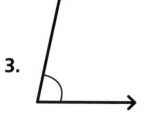 _____ right   obtuse   acute

3. 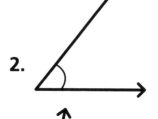 _____ right   obtuse   acute

4. 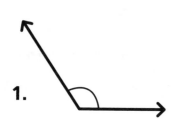 _____ right   obtuse   acute

5.  _____ right   obtuse   acute

6. 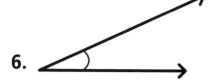 _____ right   obtuse   acute

Angle It Yourself!

Read and draw. You will need a protractor and a straightedge.

1. Draw a 45° angle.

2. Draw a 150° angle.

3. Draw a 25° angle.

4. Draw a 90° angle.

5. Draw a 135° angle.

6. Draw a 10° angle.

Ship Shape

Find the missing angles.

1. _____
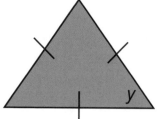

x

2. _____

y

3. _____

z

4. _____
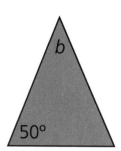

b

50°

5. _____
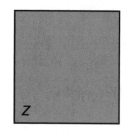

150°   n

6. _____
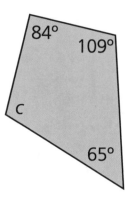

84°   109°

c

65°

Shape Up or Ship Out!

Read and draw. You will need a protractor and a straightedge.

1. Draw a parallelogram with two 140° angles and two 40° angles.

2. Draw an isosceles triangle with two 70° angles and one 40° angle.

3. Draw a square.

4. Draw an equilateral triangle.

5. Draw a quadrilateral with one 80° angle, one 70° angle, one 110° angle, and one 100° angle.

6. Draw a triangle with one 45° angle, one 60° angle, and one 75° angle.

Under Construction

Solve the problems.

1. Mrs. Murphy is making a window in her house. She wants it to be a rectangle with the perimeter of 14 feet. The length is 2 feet. What does the width need to be? What degree does each angle need to be?

_____

2. Janet is making a desk to fit in a corner. The top is an equilateral triangle. How many degrees is each angle?

_____

3. Whitney is making a drawer for the desk. It is 2 inches tall and 5 inches wide. Its volume is 120 inches^3. How long is it?

_____

4. Marcos is making a sail for his toy sailboat. It's a scalene triangle. One angle is 55°, and one is 102°. How many degrees is the third angle?

_____

5. Jeremy is making a frame for a picture. It is a square. Its perimeter is 40 inches. What is its area? What degree does each angle need to be?

_____

Super Sets

Find the mode in each set of numbers.

Find the mode in each set of numbers.

  1. _____   {2, 5, 2, 7, 2, 9}

  2. _____   {–1, 0, 1, –1}

  3. _____   {5, 10, 5, 15, 5, 20}

  4. _____   {2, 4, 2, 4, 2, 4, 2}

Find the median in each set of numbers.

  5. _____   {1, 3, 2, 5, 4}

  6. _____   {–2, 5, –4, 0, 10}

  7. _____   {10, 30, 20, 40, 0}

  8. _____   {–5, –3, 2, –9, 7}

Find the mean for each set of numbers.

  9. _____   {1, 3, 5, 7, 9}

10. _____   {6, 8, 10, 12, 14, 16}

11. _____   {–6, –3, 0, 3, 6}

12. _____   {–2, –1, 2, 4, 6, 9}

	Mode	Median	Mean
13. {5, 1, 5, 5, 4}			
14. {–2, 9, 6, –1, –2}			

Family Facts

Solve the problems.

1. Jenny is 5 feet tall. Her father is 6 feet tall. Her mother and her brother are 5.5 feet tall. What is their mean height?

_____

2. Jenny went to school 24 days in September. She went to school 23 days in October, 20 days in November, 15 days in December, and 22 days in January. Which month has the median for the number of days she went to school?

_____

3. Jenny is 12 years old. Her brother is 14. Her mother and father are 44. Her cat is 6. Find the mode, median, and mean for their ages.

_____

4. Jenny's cat ate 2 cups of food on Monday, 4 cups on Tuesday, 5 cups on Wednesday and Thursday, and 3 cups on Friday. Find the mode, median, and mean for how much food her cat ate.

_____

5. Jenny rode the bus for 4 miles in the morning. She rode it for 7 miles in the afternoon. She rode it for 4 miles at night. Find the mode, median, and mean.

_____

A Slow Finish

Make a graph with the following information.

Animal	Miles per Hour
Spider	2
Mouse	8
Chicken	9
Pig	11
Squirrel	12

Amazing Animals

Match the titles to the graphs.

Money Raised for Endangered Animals at P.S. 187
Percentage of Endangered Species for Different Groups of Animals
Favorite Animals in Mrs. Peacock's Class
How Fast Animals Go in Miles Per Hour

1. _____

_____

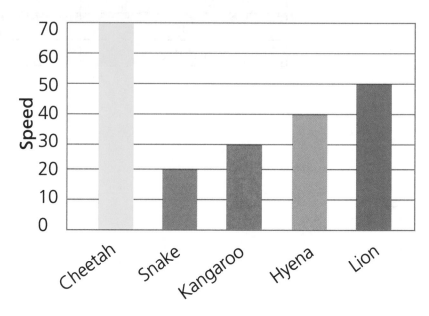

2. _____

_____

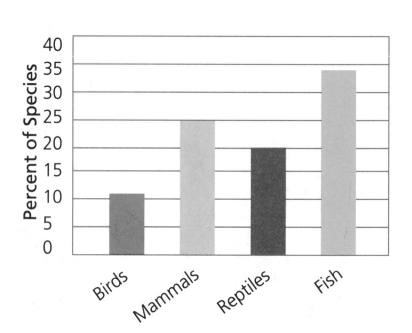

3. _____

_____

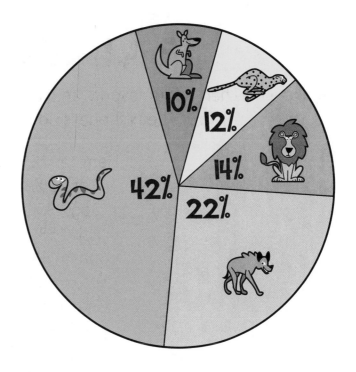

4. _____

_____

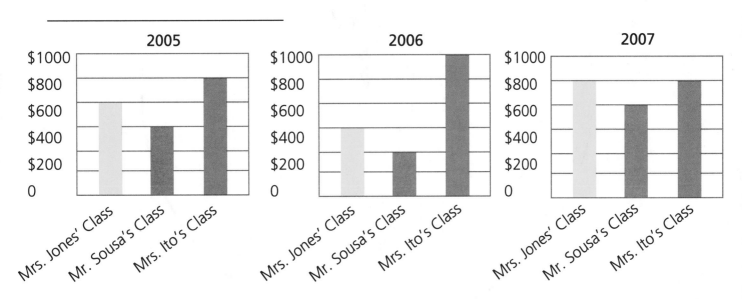

Pie Chart Pets

Make a pie chart about favorite animals. Use the information below.
The first one is done for you.

Hamster 10%
Cat 25%
Dog 13%
Fish 15%
Snake 5%
Horse 20%
Bird 12%

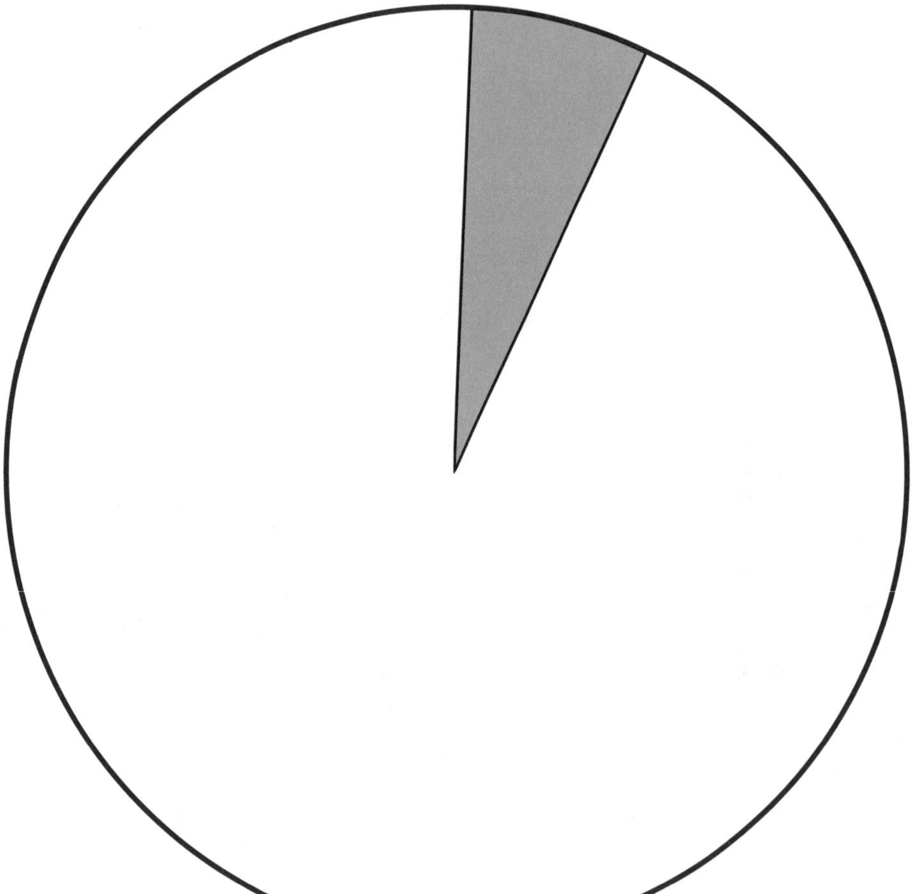

Fast, Faster, Fastest

Answer the questions. Use fractions.

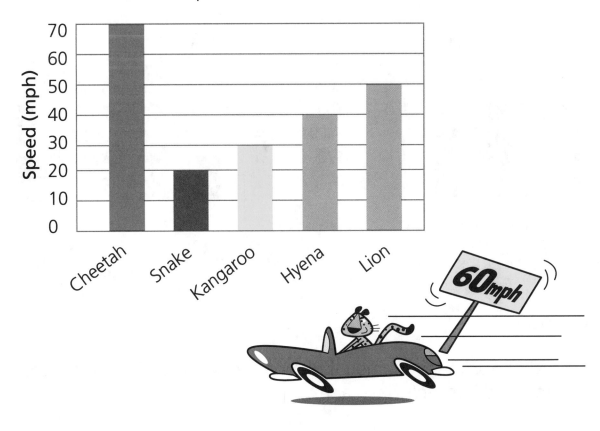

1. How many times faster does a lion run than a kangaroo?

_____

2. How many times faster does a cheetah run than a snake?

_____

3. How many times faster does a hyena run than a kangaroo?

_____

4. How many times faster does a lion run than a snake?

_____

5. How many times faster does a cheetah run than a lion?

_____

Fundraising Fun

Answer the questions. Use percents and round to the nearest whole number.

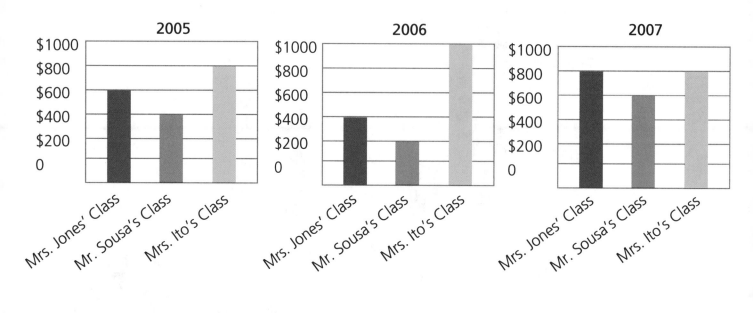

1. What was the total amount of money raised in 2005? What percentage of the total did Mrs. Ito's class raise?

_____

2. What percentage of the 2006 total did Mrs. Jones' class raise?

_____

3. What percentage of the 2007 total did Mr. Sousa's class raise?

_____

4. How much money was raised in total for all three years? What percentage of the three-year total was raised in 2005?

_____

5. What percentage of the three-year total did Mr. Sousa's class raise?

_____

Math Drill

Solve the problems and color the answers in the grid below. Some answers appear more than one time. What does it spell?

1. 25×124

2. $120 + 3{,}000$

3. $375 \div 3 =$ ___

4. $7{,}800 - 5{,}621$

5. 25% of 100 = ___

6. $\dfrac{1}{2} + \dfrac{3}{4} =$ ___

7. $\dfrac{2}{3} - \dfrac{1}{6} =$ ___

8. $2^7 \ \square \ 6^2$

9. $8^3 + 1 =$ ___

10. $.25 \ \square \ \dfrac{1}{4}$

11. $5.25 + 6.07$

12. $9.256 - 7.826$

13. $5.34 \div 3 =$ ___

14. $5.68 \times .2$

15. $9 + (-20) =$ ___

16. $(-12) - 4 =$ ___

17. $7n + 2 = 37$

$n =$ ___

18. $3a \div 4 = 6$

$a =$ ___

19. $5(4 + 10) =$ ___

20. $4(2 + 2^3) =$ ___

1.43	8	3,120	90	70	2	<	z	2,179	−2	1.78	>	602
$\frac{1}{2}$	2	$2\frac{1}{2}$	22	−11	=	225	7	5	\$	25	29.61	70
40	8	4,501	$7\frac{1}{2}$	>	0	$1\frac{1}{4}$	55	$1\frac{1}{4}$	−9	5	11	125
1.136	%	315	\$	−16	3,222	y	40	$\frac{1}{2}$	602	1.136	$\frac{3}{4}$	2,179
125	=	3,100	−2	513	<	−4	225	125	−7	11.32	−11	12.3

Answer Key

Page 4
1. 920
2. 7,040
3. 1,276
4. 2,012
5. 11,130
6. 14,911
7. 15,230
8. 93,300
9. 63,443
10. 139,360
11. 176,340
12. 800,000
13. 475,020
14. 1,161,586

Page 5
1. 14,500
2. 22,000
3. 362,000
4. 129,500
5. 389,500

Page 6
1. 874   2. 330
3. 452   4. 540
5. 2,135   6. 2,931
7. 2,400   8. 3,048
9. 1,332   10. 17,908
11. 31,327 12. 33,629
13. 39,102 14. 949,760

Page 7
1. 64,767
2. 7,475
3. 83,354
4. 1,555
5. 16,774

Page 8

Page 9

	tenth	hundredth	thousandth
1. 10.2225	10.2	10.22	10.223
2. 9.7268	9.7	9.73	9.727
3. 21.0561	21.1	21.06	21.056
4. 404.8826	404.9	404.88	404.883
5. 32.9087	32.9	32.91	32.909
6. 212.6710	212.7	212.67	212.671
7. 4.6792	4.7	4.68	4.679
8. 15.0015	15.0	15.00	15.002
9. 255.7173	255.7	255.72	255.717
10. 99.9388	99.9	99.94	99.939

Page 10
1. 38,228

2. 57,683
3. 83,458

Page 11
1. b
2. e
3. d
4. a
5. c

Page 12
1. 2,265
2. 1,592
3. 4,974
4. 0
5. 156
6. 819
7. 2,226
8. 1,340
9. 24,924
10. 35,872
11. 39,504
12. 22,378
13. 88,355
14. 211,820

Page 13
1. 3,500 pounds
2. 2,520 eggs
3. 464 calories
4. 4,890 legs
5. 20,460 pounds

Page 14
1. c
2. e
3. f
4. a
5. d
6. b

Page 15
1. 121
2. 52
3. 54 R3
4. 150 R2
5. 43 R5
6. 72
7. 300
8. 1,098 R2
9. 584 R1
10. 975
11. 46 R10
12. 26
13. 20
14. 7 R2

Page 16
1. 42 hits
2. 48 points
3. 10 minutes
4. 140 games, 35 games
5. 164 passengers, 3 passengers

Page 17

Page 18
2. 34,083; yes
3. 82,432; no
4. 170,864; no
5. 235,200; yes
6. 288,425;no
7. 690,228; yes
8. 500,610; yes

Page 19
1. 85; 100
2. 189; 200
3. 243; 200
4. 421; 400
5. 782; 800
6. 3,112; 3,100
7. 79; 100
8. 325; 300

Page 20
1. ÷   2. −
3. +   4. +
5. ÷   6. ×
7. ×   8. +
9. ÷   10. +
11. −   12. −
13. ×   14. ÷

Page 21
1. 10,868 miles
2. 2,324 miles
3. 10,916 miles
4. 94,648 miles
5. 104 miles

Page 22
1. 100
2. 75
3. 200,000
4. 300,000,000
5. 100
6. 660

Page 23
1. .50; 50%
2. .25; 25%
3. .30; 30%

4. .75; 75%
5. .62; 62%
6. .14; 14%
7. .89; 89%
8. 1.00; 100%
9. .02; 2%
10. .98; 98%
11. .28; 28%
12. .40; 40%
13. .10; 10%
14. .50; 50%

Page 24
1. 297   2. 5
3. 300   4. 55.35
5. 604.8   6. 45
7. 125   8. 385.02
9. 940   10. 660
11. 350.74   12. 3,602.40
13. 26   14. 2,460.54

Page 25
1. $6.75; $38.25
2. $57.50; $172.50
3. 25%
4. 42 books
5. 87.5%; 12.5%

Page 26
2. $\frac{15}{30} \to \frac{50}{100} \to .50 \to 50\%$
3. $\frac{6}{20} \to \frac{30}{100} \to .30 \to 30\%$
4. $\frac{41}{50} \to \frac{82}{100} \to .82 \to 82\%$

Page 27
1. >   2. >
3. =   4. >
5. <   6. >
7. >   8. =
9. <   10. >
11. =   12. >
13. =   14. >

Page 28

$3^2 \times 5$	5^4	11^2	3^9	2^4	$2^4 \times 7$	2^4
7^6	5^2	$5^2 \times 3^2$	$2^3 \times 5$	$2^9 \times 3^3$	$2^3 \times 3$	$3^3 \times 7^3$
$2^4 \times 3^3$	$5^4 \times 2$	$2^2 \times 11$	$5^4 \times 7^3$	$2^2 \times 7$	7^3	3^2
2^2	$5^2 \times 3^3$	3^2	$2^2 \times 3^2$	$2^6 \times 3^2$	2^3	$2^4 \times 3^3$
$3^4 \times 2$	$2^3 \times 3^3$	7^5	$2^2 \times 3$	11^4	5^6	$2^5 \times 3^3$
3^6	5^7	$7^4 \times 3^3$	2^5	7^3	$2^8 \times 3^2$	3^9
$2^3 \times 3^5$	$2^6 \times 3^2$	7^2	2×5^2	$2^4 \times 3$	11^3	2^3

The letter Y

Page 29
0; .34; $\frac{1}{2}$; .75; 1; $1\frac{1}{2}$; 1.66; $1\frac{3}{4}$

Page 30
1. 4.03   2. 11.45
3. 44.17   4. 112.80
5. 445.9   6. 12.588
7. 12.132   8. 10.192
9. 89.000   10. 567.448
11. 14.094   12. 70.36

13. 621.33   14. 33.503

Page 31
1. 1.6   2. 3.73
3. 2.51   4. 5.32
5. 1.5   6. 1.9
7. 60.6   8. 6.89
9. 13.78   10. 29.57
11. 32.90   12. 2.644
13. 10.597   14. 13.724

Pages 32 and 33
1. 28.8
2. 53.82
3. 6.64
4. 3.31
5. Ricardo; Wendy
6. $32.91
7. $10.53
8. $16.11
9. $61.69
10. $19.64

Page 34
1. 130   2. 30
3. 20   4. .75
5. 2.8   6. .56
7. 2.575   8. 1.27
9. 10.83   10. 25.59
11. 3.456   12. 12.05
13. 230.6   14. 28.5

Page 35
1. $47.25
2. $3.17
3. $14.25
4. $5.63
5. $59.50

Page 36

Page 37
1. 1
2. −8
3. −2
4. −20
5. −24
6. 26
7. −31
8. 57
9. −98
10. −170
11. 258
12. 282
13. −100
14. 0

Page 38
1. −8
2. −32
3. −80
4. −127
5. −86
6. −75
7. −180

8. −45
9. −297
10. −325
11. −733
12. −283
13. −529
14. −700

Page 39
1. 11
2. −86
3. −57
4. 33
5. 31
6. −109
7. −95
8. −74
9. −41
10. −45
11. −253
12. 454
13. −789
14. 246

Page 40
1. 1
2. $\frac{1}{2}$
3. $\frac{7}{10}$
4. $\frac{3}{4}$
5. $\frac{5}{8}$
6. $\frac{5}{2}$
7. $\frac{2}{7}$
8. $\frac{7}{8}$
9. $\frac{2}{5}$
10. $\frac{4}{5}$
11. $\frac{4}{6}$
12. $\frac{7}{9}$
13. $\frac{11}{12}$
14. $\frac{3}{5}$

Page 41
1. $\frac{1}{3}$
2. $\frac{2}{5}$
3. $\frac{3}{10}$
4. $\frac{1}{2}$
5. $\frac{1}{3}$
6. $\frac{3}{7}$
7. $\frac{1}{3}$
8. $\frac{1}{6}$
9. $\frac{1}{4}$
10. $\frac{1}{4}$
11. 0
12. $\frac{1}{8}$
13. $\frac{1}{2}$
14. $\frac{11}{15}$

Page 42
1. $\frac{7}{8}$
2. $\frac{2}{4}$, $\frac{1}{2}$
3. $\frac{5}{10}$, $\frac{1}{2}$
4. $\frac{6}{18}$, $\frac{3}{9}$, $\frac{1}{3}$
5. $\frac{1}{12}$
6. $\frac{10}{10}$, 1
7. $\frac{4}{6}$, $\frac{2}{3}$
8. $\frac{3}{10}$

Page 43
1. 2 cups
2. $2\frac{1}{4}$ cups
3. $12\frac{1}{4}$ cookies
4. $5\frac{2}{3}$ pieces
5. $5\frac{7}{8}$ hours

Page 44
1. $\frac{1}{12}$ more pizza

2. $1\frac{1}{3}$ more pizzas
3. $\frac{3}{8}$ more breadsticks
4. $1\frac{1}{6}$ more breadsticks
5. $2\frac{5}{12}$ more sodas

Page 45
Six cookies
$4\frac{1}{4}$, $1\frac{3}{4}$, $5\frac{3}{4}$ / $1\frac{1}{4}$, 3, 3, $1\frac{1}{2}$, $1\frac{3}{4}$, 2, $4\frac{1}{4}$

Page 46
1. $\frac{1}{8}$
2. $\frac{1}{2}$
3. $\frac{1}{5}$
4. $\frac{1}{4}$
5. $2\frac{7}{10}$
6. 1
7. 3
8. 8
9. $6\frac{1}{4}$
10. $\frac{3}{4}$
11. $3\frac{8}{9}$
12. $4\frac{1}{2}$
13. $4\frac{7}{8}$
14. $3\frac{3}{4}$

Page 47
1. 3
2. 2
3. 1
4. 2
5. $1\frac{1}{2}$
6. 6
7. $1\frac{1}{6}$
8. $1\frac{1}{5}$
9. $5\frac{1}{3}$
10. 18
11. 2
12. $1\frac{2}{5}$
13. 3
14. $2\frac{2}{9}$

Page 48
1. $\frac{3}{5}$
2. $3\frac{3}{4}$
3. $1\frac{5}{16}$
4. 6
5. $2\frac{2}{5}$
6. $6\frac{1}{2}$

Page 49
1. 3 cans
2. $23\frac{1}{3}$ cans
3. $3\frac{3}{4}$ cans
4. $6\frac{1}{8}$ hours
5. $10\frac{2}{3}$ hours

Page 50
1. $\frac{1}{2}$ hour
2. $2\frac{7}{8}$ pieces
3. $2\frac{1}{12}$ walls
4. $1\frac{1}{2}$ cans
5. $\frac{5}{12}$ hour

Page 51
1. $\frac{1}{2}$
2. $\frac{3}{4}$
3. $2\frac{1}{2}$
4. $3\frac{3}{4}$
5. $\frac{4}{5}$
6. 16
7. $5\frac{1}{4}$
8. $8\frac{1}{4}$
9. $1\frac{1}{4}$
10. $1\frac{1}{2}$

They painted four houses.

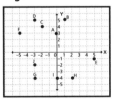

$1\frac{3}{4}$	$\frac{3}{4}$	$4\frac{3}{4}$	$5\frac{1}{4}$	$16\frac{3}{4}$
$\frac{2}{9}$	$1\frac{1}{9}$	4	$3\frac{1}{2}$	$2\frac{2}{5}$
13	16	$\frac{1}{2}$	$1\frac{3}{10}$	$\frac{1}{3}$
$5\frac{1}{2}$	7	$3\frac{1}{4}$	2	9
$\frac{3}{5}$	$\frac{1}{4}$	$2\frac{1}{2}$	$2\frac{1}{2}$	$2\frac{4}{10}$
3	$16\frac{1}{2}$	5	$\frac{4}{5}$	17

Page 52
1. 4 curtains
2. $1\frac{1}{2}$ yards
3. $6\frac{2}{3}$ yards
4. $1\frac{5}{6}$ yards
5. $9\frac{5}{12}$ yards

Page 53
6. $\frac{1}{2}$ hour
7. 7 yards
8. $5\frac{1}{4}$ feet
9. $9\frac{3}{8}$ yards
10. none; 0 yards

Page 54
1. Jupiter; 62
2. 1
3. 20
4. 26
5. 138

Page 55
1. 110 pounds
2. 60 pounds
3. Kent
4. Rocky
5. 90 pounds; 100 pounds

Page 56
1. A Museum Plan; (5,5)
2. Baseball Positions; (0,0)
3. My Neighborhood; (1,2)

Page 57
2. (3,4)   3. (4,5)
4. (6,2)   5. (6,7)
6. (9,3)

Page 58
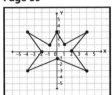

Page 59

Susie sees a star.

Page 60
1. 5   2. 4
3. 9   4. 2
5. 2   6. 50
7. 5   8. 3
9. 93   10. 6
11. 8   12. 12
13. −46   14. 9

Page 61
2. $b + 5 = 20$; $b = 15$
3. $20 + m = 60$; $m = 40$
4. $6b + 5 = 53$; $b = 8$
5. $14 + (-2) + b = 24$; $b = 12$

Page 62
2. No (crossed out)
3. Yes (circled)
4. No (crossed out)
5. No (crossed out)
6. Yes (circled)
7. No (crossed out)
8. No (crossed out)
9. Yes (circled)
10. No (crossed out)
Diego went to the park.

Page 63
1. 48   2. 100
3. 242   4. 198
5. 180   6. 1,573
7. 396   8. 57
9. 72   10. 1,650
11. 126   12. 270
13. 42   14. 40

Page 64
2. $6 \times 37 \rightarrow (6 \times 30) + (6 \times 7) \rightarrow$
   $180 + 42 \rightarrow 222$
3. $4 \times 15 \rightarrow (4 \times 10) + (4 \times 5) \rightarrow$
   $40 + 20 \rightarrow 60$
4. $8 \times 37 \rightarrow (8 \times 30) + (8 \times 7) \rightarrow$
   $240 + 56 \rightarrow 296$

Page 65
1. 9
2. 10
3. 3
4. 2
5. 100
6. 7
7. 7
8. 16
9. 9
10. 3
11. 106
12. 8
13. 67
14. 20

Page 66
1. $x + y = 2$

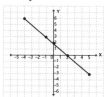

Page 67
2. $2x + 1 = y$

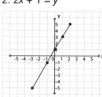

Page 68

x	y
−2	−3
−1	1
0	5
1	9
3	17

x	y
−9	−6
−6	−4
3	2
6	4
9	6

x	y
−5	−8
−3	−4
0	2
2	6
12	26

x	y
−4	−28
−2	−14
1	7
4	28
10	70

Page 69

(−1, 1)	(0, 6)	(0, 0)	(2, −13)	(−3, −7)
(−5, 15)	(0, 5)	(1, −9)	(2, 13)	(3, 7)
(−6, −20)	(7, 31)	(−4, −11)	(3, −7)	(−9, 30)
(−2, −3)	(3, 17)	(2, 20)	(−10, −35)	(9, 1)
(5, 25)	(1, 1)	(4, 17)	(5, 0)	(1, 9)

X marks the spot where Sandra will find the treasure.

Page 70
1. 32 in.   2. 28 in.
3. 14 in.   4. 21 in.
5. 46 cm   6. 96 cm
7. 38 cm   8. 12 ft.
9. 18 ft.

Page 71
The following shapes are colored: 2, 4, 5, 7, 8.

Page 72
1. 2,704 ft.^{2} > 2,112 ft.^{2}
2. 9 ft.^{2} = 9 ft.^{2}
3. 35 ft.^{2} < 36 ft.^{2}

Page 73
4. 10 yd.^{2} < 48 yd.^{2}
5. 2,420 ft.^{2} = 2,420 ft.^{2}
6. 34 ft.^{2} > 31.5 ft.^{2}

Pages 74 and 75
1. 60 feet^3 2. 120 inches^3
3. 96 cm^3 4. 24 feet^3
5. 60 inches^3 6. 16 feet^3

Page 76

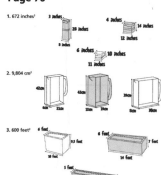

1. 672 inches^3
2. 9,804 cm^3
3. 600 feet^3

Page 77
1. 54 ft.   2. 126 ft.^{2}
3. 1,008 ft.^{3} 4. 162 ft.
5. 6 ft.^{2}

Page 78

Page 79
Students draw lines the correct length.

Page 80
1. 120°; obtuse   2. 55°; acute
3. 80°; acute   4. 90°; right
5. 175°; obtuse   6. 30°; acute

Page 81

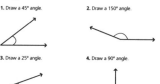

1. Draw a 45° angle.
2. Draw a 150° angle.
3. Draw a 25° angle.
4. Draw a 90° angle.
5. Draw a 135° angle.
6. Draw a 10° angle.

Page 82
1. 90°   2. 60°
3. 90°   4. 80°
5. 30°   6. 102°

Page 83

1. Draw a parallelogram with two 140° angles and two 40° angles.
2. Draw an isosceles triangle with two 70° angles and one 40° angle.
3. Draw a square.
4. Draw an equilateral triangle.
5. Draw a quadrilateral with one 80° angle, one 70° angle, one 110° angle, and one 100° angle.
6. Draw a triangle with one 45° angle, one 60° angle, and one 75° angle.

Page 84
1. 5 feet; 90°
2. 60°
3. 12 inches
4. 23°
5. 100 inches^2; 90°

Page 85
1. 2   2. −1
3. 5   4. 2
5. 3   6. 0
7. 20   8. −3
9. 5   10. 11
11. 0   12. 3
13. 5, 5, 4   14. −2, −1, 2

Page 86
1. 5.5 feet
2. January
3. mode = 44, median = 14, mean = 24
4. mode = 5, median = 4, mean = 3.8
5. mode = 4, median = 4, mean = 5

Page 87

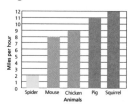

Page 88
1. How Fast Animals Go in Miles Per Hour
2. Percentage of Endangered Species Animals for Different Groups of Animals

Page 89
3. Favorite Animals in Mrs. Peacock's Class
4. Money Raised for Endangered Animals at P.S. 187

Page 90

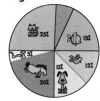

Page 91
1. $1\frac{2}{3}$ times faster
2. $3\frac{1}{2}$ times faster
3. $1\frac{1}{3}$ times faster
4. $2\frac{1}{2}$ times faster
5. $1\frac{2}{5}$ times faster

Page 92
1. $1,800; 44%
2. 25%
3. 27%
4. $5,600; 32%
5. 21%

Page 93
1. 3,100   2. 3,120   3. 125
4. 2,179   5. 25   6. $1\frac{1}{4}$
7. $\frac{1}{2}$ 8. >   9. 513
10. =   11. 11.32   12. 1.43
13. 1.78   14. 1.136   15. −11
16. −16   17. 5   18. 8
19. 70   20. 40

1.43	8	3,120	90	70	2	<	z	2,179	−2	1.78	>	602
$\frac{1}{2}$	2	$2\frac{1}{4}$	22	−11	=	225	7	5	$	25	29.61	70
40	8	4,501	$7\frac{1}{2}$	>	0	$1\frac{1}{4}$	55	$1\frac{1}{2}$	−9	5	11	125
1.136	%	315	5	−16	3,222	y	40	$	602	1.136	$\frac{1}{2}$	2,179
125	=	3,100	−2	513	<	−4	225	125	−7	11.32	−11	12.3

It spells "end."